SAINT
BRIDE

SAINT BRIDE

EDITED AND PRESENTED
BY IAIN MACDONALD

FLORIS BOOKS

First published in 1992 by Floris Books

British Library CIP Data available

ISBN 0-86315-142-6

Printed in Great Britain
by Courier International, East Kilbride

Contents

Introduction

The historical St Bride of Kildare, otherwise known as Brigid or Brigit, lived in the fifth century, was a contemporary of St Patrick, and founder of a great community of nuns. More than that, it is almost impossible to say with any sure foundation. However, there can be little doubt of the impact and revelation of her life on the people of Ireland, and, after her death, her reputation quickly spread into Scotland and northern England, as well.

St Bride lived through the momentous transition from pagan to Christian Ireland and the new Church seems to have happily superimposed her image over that of an older pagan mother goddess of a similar name and with like associations. A related deity, known as Brigantia, was revered by the Brigantes of northern England, and a parallel conversion and adoption there may partly account for the cult of St Bride spreading so rapidly outside Ireland.

With pagan and Christian elements so closely intermingled, most of the documents which have come down to us reflect the difficulty of distinguishing between them. Some accounts tell us that as a newly born child, Bride was bathed in milk, and henceforth could eat no mortal food but only the milk of a white,

red-eared cow. Elements such as these are known to
have pagan origins, as does the charming story of how
Bride once hung her wet robe to dry on a ray of the
sun.

But where does pagan myth stop and Christian
legend begin? Baptized and named by angels, Bride
restored the dead to life, healed the sick and made the
dumb speak. She turned water into ale and cursed an
apple tree which became barren. She worked miracles
of plenty. Her girdle, even her shadow, had healing
powers. She saw into the souls of others, and
confronted the Devil. Elements such as these at least
appear to be Christian, as are later legends that Bride
was the midwife of the Virgin Mary, and godmother
to the Child Jesus.

But Bride is also the guardian of the poor pastoral
folk who work the land: she protects the harvest; she
increases the yield of cow and sheep. She lights the fire
which is never extinguished, the ever-burning fire in
the hearth of the humble croft. In all this, we hear
echoes of more ancient associations, similarly in the
fact that Bride is the patron of studies and learning,
just as the older Celtic goddess Brigid succoured the
arts and poetry.

For our world today, Bride has special importance
perhaps for being, in Alice Curtayne's words, "the
most celebrated Irishwoman of all time." Bride was a

*wealthy lord's daughter by a bondmaid, and according
to the custom of the time, belonged body and soul to
her master. But she was marked from her birth as a
child of special destiny and was never sold in bondage,
though her mother was. Bride dedicated herself as a
free woman to the religious life and, when the time
came for her to take the veil from Bishop Mél:*

> *it came to pass then, through the grace of the Holy
> Spirit, that the form of ordaining a bishop was
> read out over Brigid. Mac-caille said that a
> bishop's order should not be conferred on a
> woman. Bishop Mél said: "No power have I in
> this matter. That dignity has been given by God
> unto Brigid, beyond every other woman."
> Wherefore the men of Ireland from that time to
> this give episcopal honour to Brigid's successor.*

*The achievement and authority ascribed to Bride seem
to place her in a quite unique role in her own troubled
times, sought out by kings and princes for their
security and protection. The ninth century poem
"Hail Brigid," included in this book, gives eloquent
expression to her temporal, as well as spiritual,
powers.*

*Perhaps in recognition of Bride as one of the most
potent symbols of Christian womanhood for all times,
her saintly glory is suffused in legend with her role as
"the Bride of Christ," and at times confused almost*

*with the identity of the Virgin Mother herself. The
wonderful peroration of the* Life of Brigid *in the*
Book of Lismore *ends thus: "She is the prophetess
of Christ; she is the Queen of the South; she is the
Mary of the Gael."*

The life of Brigid

*In 1814, workmen engaged in repairs at Lismore
Castle, in Co. Waterford, came across a walled up
passage where they found a wooden box. In the box
was a crozier and an old manuscript copied on vellum,
with many pages missing and those remaining much
damaged by damp, rats and mice.*

The so-called Book of Lismore *turned out to
contain lives, written in Irish, of ancient Irish saints.
It appears to have been compiled from the lost* Book
of Monasterboice *and other manuscripts, in the
fifteenth century. The original scribes, from the
evidence of their work, took little care and displayed
great ignorance about what they were copying. Added
to the problems of fading, damp and downright error,
later unskilful attempts to rewrite parts of the*

manuscript only increased the difficulty of interpreta-
tion. Because of these obstacles, much scholarly labour
was needed to establish a viable text. In 1890,
Whitley Stokes published his edited version and
translation of the Lives of the Saints from the
Book of Lismore, on which the present text is
based.

The Life of Brigid corresponds closely with two
other surviving lives of Bride: the Tertia Vita
included in John Colgan's collected lives in the Trias
Thaumaturga of 1647; and the tenth century Irish
life of the Lebar Brecc which Whitley Stokes printed
with a translation in Three Middle-Irish Homilies
in 1877. The Tertia Vita is thought to predate
another life written by Cogitosus in the seventh
century, so it would appear that the root sources of the
life in the Book of Lismore are fairly ancient.

Writing the "life" of a saint in pre-medieval times
was clearly not the same sort of activity as it would be
today. To begin with, few, if any, written records
were available and the hagiographer would have to
rely a great deal on oral tradition. It is obvious from
the present life that the mists of time had already
started to close thickly around the historical figure of
St Bride. But most lives of this kind were written as
aids to devotion, rather than as historical accounts.
The writer gives little or no hint as to the chronology

of events: there is a birth, there is a death, and in between there is a whole host of tales, legends, myths and anecdotes. We do not therefore need to look for facts, but rather for the spirit of the saint upon the land.

For the sake of readability, some modernization of Whitley Stokes' text has been imposed, together with various minor changes and deletions. The "Hymn to St Brigid," ascribed to St Columba among others, has been placed at the end of the text in this edition.

Hi sunt qui sequuntur Agnum quocumque ierit.
It is these that follow the Lamb wherever he goes.
(John: 14.4)

his is to follow the Lamb: to imitate Christ and to follow Him by fulfilling the Law and the Gospel, without the desire of earthly things, without the love for perishable things, to avoid honour, to despise the world, to be profitable to all, never to do injustice or wrong to anyone, patiently to suffer temptations from without, to grant forgiveness to the persecutors: that every good thing that one doth be done for the magnifying of God and not for the glorifying of oneself.

Imitate then, as the wise man says, as is the undefiled Lamb in the virginity of the flesh, so is the undefiled body of the Son of the Heavenly Father. Imitate then the mystical Lamb, even Christ, in virginity and holiness of mind, as He himself said: *Abide holily and chastely,* said the Lord, *for I am holy and I am innocent.* For the chastity of the body is not the better, if the soul is imperfect and defiled."

Now a multitude of holy and righteous men fulfilled this commandment of virginity, even as the holy maiden fulfilled it, for whom there is a festival and commemoration on the occurrence of this season and time, that is St Brigid, the virgin of the Lord of the Elements.

Here, then, is related something of the miracles and marvels of the holy Brigid, and of her genealogy: namely, Brigid, daughter of Dubthach, son of Demre, son of Bresal, of the sept of Echaid Find Fuathnairt.

That same Dubthach bought a bondmaid named Broicsech. She was a daughter of Dallbrónach of Dál Conchobair in the south of Bregia. Dubthach joined himself in wedlock to that bondmaid, and she became with child by him. Jealousy of the bondmaid seized Dubthach's wife, and she said to him: "Unless thou sellest this bondmaid in distant lands, I will exact my dowry from thee and I will leave thee." However Dubthach did not desire to sell the bondmaid.

Once he and the bondmaid along with him went in a chariot past the house of a certain wizard. When the wizard heard the noise of the chariot he said: "My boy," said he, "see who is in the chariot, for this is noise of chariot under king."

Then said the boy:"Dubthach is in the chariot."

The wizard went to meet them, and asked whose was the woman who was biding in the chariot.

"Mine," said Dubthach.

Now Maithgen was the name of the wizard, and from him Ross Maithgin is named. The wizard asked if she was pregnant by anyone.

"She is pregnant by me," said Dubthach.

Then the wizard said: "Marvellous will be the child that is in her womb: her like will not be on earth."

"My wife compels me," said Dubthach, "to sell this bondmaid."

Said the wizard through grace of prophecy: "The seed of thy wife shall serve the seed of the bondmaid, for the bondmaid will bring forth a daughter conspicuous, radiant, who will shine like a sun among the stars of heaven."

Dubthach was thankful for that answer, for till then no daughter had been born to him.

Then they went to their house, and both gave thanks. Well known, now, was the love that God had for that virgin. For two bishops of the Britons, named Mél and Melchu, came from Scotland to prophesy of her and to bless her. Dubthach gave them a welcome, and the bondmaid did attend and serve upon them. Sad and mournful was Dubthach's wife. Bishop Mél asked her the cause of her sadness. The woman said to him: "Because Dubthach prefers his bondmaid to me."

Said Bishop Mél: "Reason has he though he should prefer her, for thy seed shall serve the bondmaid's, but her seed shall be profitable to thine."

She was angry at that. Then there came to Dubthach's house a poet of Hni Meic Uais from gathering treasures. When the poet knew the cause of the woman's anger, he asked: "Sellest thou the handmaid?"

"I will sell," said Dubthach, "for I must needs do so."

The bishops said: "Sell the bondmaid, but do not sell the offspring."

He did as they said and the poet left with his new bondmaid. Now on the night that the poet reached his home, a holy man happened to be in the house entreating the Lord and praying. To him was manifested a flame and a fiery pillar rising from the place where the bondmaid was biding.

A certain wizard went from Tirconnell to the house of the poet and he bought the service of the bondmaid. The poet sold him the bondmaid, and did not sell the offspring that lay in her womb. The wizard went home with his bondmaid.

Then it came to pass that the wizard made a great feast, and bade the king of Conaille to the feast; and it was then the time for the king's wife to bring forth a child. There was a soothsayer along with the king, and a friend of the king's asked him when it would be lucky for the queen to bring forth.

The wizard said: "that the child which should be brought forth on the morrow at sunrise, and neither within the house nor without, would outgo every child in Ireland."

Now the queen's lying-in came before that

hour, and she brought forth a dead son. But on the morrow, when the bondmaid went at sunrise with a vessel full of milk in her hand, and when she put one of her two footsteps over the threshold of the house, the other foot being inside, then she brought forth the daughter, even St Brigid. The maidservants washed St Brigid with the milk that was still in her mother's hand. Now that was in accord with Brigid's merit, even with the brightness and sheen of her chastity. The girl was taken straightway after her birth to the queen's dead son, and when the girl's breath came to the son, he arose out of death.

Thus the wizard went with his bondmaid and her daughter into the province of Connaught, for her mother was of Connaught, but her father of Munster.

On a certain day the bondmaid went to milk her kine, and left the girl alone sleeping in her house. Certain neighbours beheld the house, wherein the girl lay, ablaze, so that one flame was made thereof from earth to heaven. When they came to rescue the house, there was no fire, but they saw that the girl was full of the grace of the Holy Spirit.

One day the wizard was sitting with his

handmaid in a certain place, and the cow-dung which lay before the girl they beheld ablaze. When they stretched their hands out to it, there was no fire.

Once when the wizard was sleeping, he saw three clerics in shining garments, who poured oil on the girl's head; and they completed the order of baptism in the usual manner. Those were three angels. Said the third angel to the wizard, that the name of the girl was *Sancta Brigida,* that is, St Brigid. The wizard arose and related what he had beheld.

One day the infant's voice was heard crying, and this she said: *Meum erit hoc,* that is, this will be mine. When the wizard heard that, he said: "What the girl declares will be fulfilled," that is, the land will be mine afterwards, and this has been fulfilled. When the people of that land heard this they ordered the wizard out of the country, so he went to his own patrimony.

Now this holy virgin Brigid was reared on food different from that of children of her own age, for she was more ... than every infant. She would not consume unclean food. She rejected the wizard's food, and used to throw it up. The wizard meditated why the girl was thus. It appeared to him that it was because of the

corruption and impurity of his food. Then he
entrusted a red-eared cow to give milk separate-
ly to Brigid, and he let a faithful woman milk
her. The holy girl used to consume that milk,
and did not throw it up.

Then this holy virgin was reared till she was a
handmaid. And everything to which her hand
was set used to increase. She tended the sheep,
she satisfied the birds, she fed the poor. When
boldness, and strength and size came to Brigid,
she desired to go and visit her fatherland. The
wizard sent messages to Dubthach, that he
should come to meet his daughter. The messen-
gers went to Dubthach, and related the maiden's
miracles and marvels. Dubthach came, and was
joyous. The wizard made him welcome, and
gave his daughter to him free.

Then Dubthach and Brigid went to their
country in the province of Offaly. And her
nurse was along with Brigid, and illness seized
her nurse as she was wending her way. So
Brigid and another girl were sent to ask a drink
of ale for her from a certain man named
Baethchu, who was making a mighty feast. He
refused Brigid. Then Brigid went to a nearby
well, and filled her vessel from it and blessed the
water, so that it turned into the taste of ale, and

she gave it to her nurse, who straightway became whole. As to the feast at which she was refused, when they went to drink, not a drop of ale was found.

nce when Dubthach went on a journey, he left his daughter with his swine. And two robbers came to her, and carried off two boars of the herd. When they had gone a little while after that Dubthach met them. He took the swine from them, and then he came to Brigid.

"Do the swine remain, my girl?" said Dubthach.

"Count them," said Brigid. Dubthach counted the swine, and not one of them was lacking.

Not long after that came a noble guest to Dubthach's house, and hospitality was shewn to them, and five pieces of bacon were given to Brigid to be boiled.

And a miserable hungry hound came into the house to Brigid. Brigid out of pity gave him the fifth piece of bacon. The hound was not satisfied with that. So Brigid gave him another piece. She thought that the guest was asleep, but this was

not so. Then came Dubthach and said to Brigid:
"Hast thou boiled the bacon? and do the
portions remain?"

"Count them," said she. Dubthach counted
them. Not one of them was wanting. The guest
told Dubthach what Brigid had done. The
guests did not consume that food, for they were
unworthy of it; but it was dealt out to the poor
and needy.

Once a certain faithful woman invited Brigid to
go with her into Moy Liffey; for a gathering of
the synod of Leinster was held there. It was
manifested to Bishop Ibhair, who was in the
assembly, that Mary the Virgin was coming into
the assembly. The woman went on the morrow,
Brigid being alone with her, into the assembly.
Then said Bishop Ibhair: "This is the Mary
whom I beheld;" and the whole gathering
blessed St Brigid. Wherefore Brigid is henceforth called "the Mary of the Gael."

Afterwards Brigid went to visit her mother
who was in bondage. Thus was her mother, in
sickness before her, and she was at a mountain-
dairy having twelve cows with her, and she
collecting butter. Now the virgin served hum-
bly after her mother, and began setting the dairy

to rights. The churning that was made was
divided into twelve portions in honour of the
Lord's twelve apostles. And the thirteenth portion was set so that in honour of Christ it was
greater than every other portion, and it was
given to the poor and to the guests. For she used
to say that Christ was in the person of every
faithful guest. That seemed a marvel to the
neatherd, and he went to converse with the
wizard.

The wizard and his wife asked: "Has the
virgin cared well for the dairy?"

Then he came to the kine. "It is well," said the
neatherd, "I am thankful anyhow, and the calves
are fat." For he did not dare to blame Brigid in
her absence. The wizard and his wife went to the
dairy, having with them a great hamper eight-
een hands high to be filled with butter. Brigid
made them welcome, and washed their feet, and
gave them food.

Then said the wizard's wife to Brigid: "We
have come hither to know whether that which
has been entrusted to thee has profited. Of
butter, what hast thou?"

None in readiness had she save the making of
one churning and a half. Then Brigid went into
the kitchen, and this she said:

Oh, my Prince,
Who canst do all these things,
Bless, O God — a cry unforbidden —
My kitchen with thy right hand!

My kitchen,
The kitchen of the white God,
A kitchen which my King has blessed,
A kitchen that has butter.

Mary's Son, my Friend, cometh
To bless my kitchen.
My Prince, even to the ends of the earth,
May we have abundance with him!

And she brought the half making of her churning from the back of the kitchen. The wizard's wife mocked at this and said: "This quantity of butter is good to fill a large hamper!"

"Fill your hamper," said Brigid, "and God will put something therein."

She still kept going into her kitchen, and bringing out half a making every time, and singing a stave of those staves as she went back. If the hampers which the men of Munster possessed had been given to her, she would have filled them all. The wizard and his wife marvelled at the miracle which they beheld.

Then the wizard said to Brigid: "This butter and the kine which thou hast milked, I offer to thee; and thou shalt not be serving me, but serve the Lord."

Said Brigid: "Take the kine, and give me my mother's freedom."

The wizard said: "Behold thy mother free for thee, and the kine; and whatsoever thou shalt say, that will I do."

Then Brigid dealt out the kine to the poor and the needy; and the wizard was baptized, and he was full of faith; and he remained till his death in Brigid's company.

Thereafter Brigid went with her mother to her father's house. Of her father's wealth and food and property, whatsoever her hands would find or would get, she used to give to the poor and needy of the Lord. Wherefore her father was displeased with her and desired to sell the holy Brigid. He and his daughter along with him went in a chariot, and he said: "Not for honour or for reverence to thee art thou carried in the chariot; but to take thee to sell thee, that thou mayst grind at the quern of Dunlaing, son of Enna, king of Leinster."

When they came to the king's fortress, Dubthach went into the fortress to the king, and left his sword near Brigid in the chariot. And a leper came to Brigid, and besought Brigid in God's name to bestow something upon him. Brigid handed him down her father's sword.

Dubthach said to the king after he had come inside: "Wilt thou buy my daughter from me?"

"Wherefore sellest thou thine own daughter?" said Dunlaing.

"Not hard to say," said Dubthach. "It is because she is selling my wealth, and bestowing it on wretched worthless men."

"Let her be brought to us that we may see her," said Dunlaing.

Dubthach went for her. When he came he was looking at the chariot and he saw not his sword. He asked Brigid what she had done with his sword.

"I gave it," said Brigid, "to a poor man who came to beg of me."

Dubthach was mightily enraged with her for having given the sword away. When Brigid came before the king, he said: "Why dost thou steal thy father's property and wealth, and, what is worse, why hast thou given the sword away?"

Then said Brigid: "The Virgin's Son knoweth, if I had thy power, with all thy wealth, and with all thy Leinster, I would give them all to the Lord of the Elements."

Said the king to Dubthach: "It is not meet for us to deal with this maiden, for her merit before God is higher than ours."

Thus was Brigid saved from bondage.

ot long after there came a certain man of good kin to Dubthach to ask for his daughter in marriage. Dubthach and his sons were willing, but Brigid refused. A brother of her brethren said to her: "Idle is the pure eye in thy head, not to be on a bolster beside a husband."

Brigid said: "The Son of the Virgin knoweth, it is not healthy for us if it bring harm upon us."

Then she put her finger under the eye and plucked it out of her head, so that it lay on her cheek. When Dubthach and her brethren beheld that, they promised that she should never be told to go to a husband save the husband whom she should like. Then Brigid put her palm to her eye, and it was healed at once.

Brigid and certain virgins along with her went to take the veil from Bishop Mél in Telcha

Mide. He was content to see them. For humility Brigid held back so that she might be the last to whom the veil was given. But a fiery pillar rose from her head to the roof-ridge of the church.

Then said Bishop Mél: "Come forward, O holy Brigid, that a veil may be sained on thy head before the other virgins."

It came to pass then, through the grace of the Holy Ghost, that the form of ordaining a bishop was read out over Brigid. Mac-caille said that a bishop's order should not be conferred on a woman.

Bishop Mél said: "No power have I in this matter. That dignity has been given by God unto Brigid, beyond every other woman."

Wherefore the men of Ireland from that time to this give episcopal honour to Brigid's successor.

On the eighth of the month Brigid was born, on a Thursday; on the eighteenth she took the veil; in the eighty-eighth year of her age she went to heaven. With eight virgins was Brigid consecrated, according to the number of the eight beatitudes of the Gospel which she fulfilled, and of them all it was the beatitude of mercy that Brigid chose.

Once when the high tide of Easter drew nigh, she desired through charity to brew ale for the many churches that were around her. And there was a scarcity of corn at that time in Meath, and Brigid had only one sieve of malt. Brigid's household, moreover, had no vessels save two troughs. They put the malt into one of the two troughs. They filled the other vessel with the ale. Then the ale was distributed by Brigid to seventeen churches of Fir Tulach, so that the produce of one measure of malt supplied them through Brigid's grace from Maundy Thursday to Low Sunday.

Once there came a certain leper unto Brigid to ask for a cow. Brigid said to him: "Which seemeth best to thee, to take away a cow or to be healed of the leprosy?"

The leper said that he would rather be healed of the leprosy than be given the kingdom of the world. Brigid made prayer to God and healed the leper, and he afterwards served Brigid.

A certain nun of Brigid's household fell into sore disease and desired milk. There did not happen to be a cow in the church at that time, so a vessel was filled with water for Brigid, and she blessed it, and it was turned into milk. She gave it to the nun who at once became quite well.

Now when the fame and renown of Brigid had gone throughout Ireland, there came to Brigid two blind men of the Britons and a leper to be healed. Said Brigid: "Stay outside at present till the celebration be over." Said the Britons, for they were impatient: "Thou healedst folk of thine own kin yesterday, and thou hast not waited to heal us today."

Brigid made prayer, and the three of them were healed at once.

When the hightide of Easter was fulfilled, Brigid asked of her maidens whether they still had the leavings of the Easter ale. The maidens replied: "God will give," said they. Then came in two maidens having a pail full of water.

"The Virgin's Son knoweth," said Brigid, "that there is good ale there."

It seemed to her that it was ale. As she said that, the water was straightway changed into choice ale. It was afterwards given to Bishop Mél, and also to the virgins.

At the same time came a disease of the eyes to Brigid, and her head seemed exceeding weary. When Bishop Mél heard of that he said: "Let us go together to seek a physician, that thou mayest have thy head cured."

Said Brigid: "If thou hadst not been disobedient, I should not have desired any bodily physician; however we will do what thou shalt say."

As they were faring forth, Brigid fell out of her chariot and her head came against a stone, and she was greatly wounded and the blood gushed out. Then with that blood were healed two dumb women who were lying on the road. After that, the leech whom they were seeking chanced to meet them. When he saw the wound he said: "Thou shouldst not seek any other physician from this time forward, save the Physician who healed thee on this occasion; for though all the doctors of Ireland should be doctoring thee, they could do nothing better."

So in that wise Brigid was healed.

Once the king of Teffia came into their neighbourhood for a banquet. There was a covered vessel in the king's hand. A certain incautious man took it out of his hand, and it fell and broke into fragments. The man was seized by the king. Bishop Mél went to plead for him, and nought was got from the king save his death-sentence. So Bishop Mél begged for the broken vessel, and took it with him to Brigid. Then Brigid breathed round it, and it was renewed in a form

that was better than before. Then it was taken
back to the king, and the captive was released.
And Bishop Mél said: "Not for me has God
wrought this miracle, but for Brigid."

Once Brigid went to the house of another
virgin, Brigid daughter of Conaille. The water
that was put over Brigid's feet after she had
arrived, healed a certain virgin who was lying
sick in the house. Now when Brigid with her
virgins went to eat their dinner, she began to
look for a long while at the table. The other
Brigid asked, "What perceivest thou?"

Brigid said, "I see the Devil on the table."

"I should like to see him," said the other
virgin.

"Make Christ's Cross on thy face, and on thy
eyes," said Brigid.

The virgin made it, and she beheld Satan
beside the table, his head down and his feet up,
his smoke and his flame out of his gullet, and
out of his nose.

Brigid said: "Give answer to us, O Devil!"

"I cannot, O Nun," said the Demon, "refuse
to answer thee, for thou art a keeper of God's
commandments, and thou art merciful to the
poor and to the Lord's household."

"Tell us then," said Brigid: "why hast thou come to us among our nuns?"

"There is a certain pious virgin here," said the Devil, "and in her companionship am I, enjoining upon her sloth and negligence."

Brigid said to that virgin: "Put the Cross of Christ over thy face, and over thine eyes."

She put it at once and the virgin beheld the hideous monster. Great fear seized the virgin when she beheld the demon.

Brigid said to her: "Why dost thou shun the fosterling whom thou hast been tending for so long a time?"

The virgin then made repentance and was healed of the demon.

certain woman brought unto Brigid a hamper full of apples. Then lepers came to Brigid begging for apples. Brigid said: "Give the apples to them."

When the woman heard that, she took back; her hamper of apples, and said: "To thee thyself I brought the apples, and not to lepers."

It was an annoyance to Brigid that her alms should be forbidden, and she cursed the trees from which it had been brought. When the woman went home, she found not a single apple in her barn, although it had been full when she left, and the trees were barren thenceforward.

Once Brigid went to Teffia with great hosts accompanying her; and there were two lepers behind her between whom a dispute arose. When one of the lepers desired to smite the other, his hand withered and the hand of the other of them shrank. Then they repented, and Brigid healed them of their leprosy.

Brigid went to a certain church in the land of Teffia to celebrate Easter. The prioress of the church said to her maidens that on Maundy Thursday one of them should minister unto the old men and to the weak and feeble persons who were biding in the church. Not one of them was found for the ministering. Then Brigid said: "I today will minister unto them."

There were four of the sick persons who were biding in the church: a consumptive man, and a lunatic, and a blind man, and a leper. And Brigid did service to these four, and they were healed from every disease that lay upon them.

Once Brigid went into a certain house as a guest.
It came to pass that all the household went forth
except one little consumptive lad, and he was
dumb, and Brigid knew not that he was so.
Then came guests unto Brigid into the house to
beg for food. Brigid asked of this dumb lad,
where was the key of the kitchen. Said the lad:
"I know the place in which it is."

Brigid said: "Go and fetch it to me."

He rose at once and attended on the guests.

Then came to pass an assembly of the men of
Ireland in Teltown, a stead wherein were Patrick
and the synod of Ireland along with him. Brigid
and Bishop Mél went to the meeting, and they
found a difficult case before them in the
meeting: to wit, a certain woman brought forth
a child there, and said that the child was by
Bishop Brón, one of Patrick's household.
Bishop Brón denied that the child was by
him.

That question was brought to Brigid to be
resolved. Brigid asked the woman by whom she
had conceived the child, and told her not to utter
falsehood. Said the woman: "It is by Bishop
Brón."

Tumour and swelling filled her tongue in her
head, so that she was unable to speak. Brigid

made the sign of the Cross over the infant's mouth, and asked: "Who is thy father?"

The infant answered: "A wretched, miserable man who is in the outskirts of the assembly, that is my father."

Thus Bishop Brón was saved by Brigid's favour.

hen came a man for Brigid to ask that she might go to consecrate a new house which had been built for him. When he had prepared food for Brigid, Brigid said to her maidens: "It is not lawful for us to eat the food of this heathen man, for God has revealed to me that he has never been baptized."

When the goodman heard that, grief of heart seized him, and Bishop Brón baptized him. Thereafter Patrick ordered Brigid and his successor that they should never be without an ordained person in their company: therefore Nat-fraich took priest's orders.

At the same time a man from the south of Bregia bore his mother on his back to Brigid to be healed, for she was consumptive; and he put her from his back on Brigid's shadow, and when the shadow touched her, she was whole at once.

At another time they saw Patrick coming to them. Lassair said to Brigid: "What shall we do for the multitude that has come to us?"

"What food have ye?" asked Brigid.

"There is nought," said Lassair, "save one sheep, and twelve loaves, and a little milk."

Said Brigid: "That is good: the preaching of God's word will be made unto us and we shall be satisfied thereby."

When Patrick had finished the preaching, the food was brought to Brigid that she might divide it. And she blessed it; and the two peoples of God, even Brigid's congregation and Patrick's congregation, were satisfied; and their leavings were much more than the material that had been there at first.

There was a certain man biding in Lassair's church, and his wife was leaving him and would neither eat nor sleep along with him; so he came to Brigid to ask for a spell to make his wife love him.

Brigid blessed water for him and said: "Put that water over the house, and over the food, and over the drink of yourselves, and over the bed in your wife's absence."

When he had done thus, the wife gave exceeding great love to him, so that she could

not keep apart from him, even on one side of the
house; but she was always at one of his hands.
He went one day on a journey and left the wife
asleep. When the woman awoke she rose up
lightly and went after the husband, and saw him
afar from her, with an arm of the sea between
them. She cried out to her husband and said that
she would go into the sea unless he came to her.

A certain woman of Hni Meic Uais came to
Brigid to beg; and before that she had always
been in poverty. So Brigid gave her girdle to
her, and Brigid said that it would heal whatsoever disease or illness to which it was applied.
And it was so done, and thus the woman used to
make her livelihood thenceforward.

Once on a certain high feast, friends came to
Brigid, having with them an offering, and they
had left their house behind them without care-
takers. Thereafter came robbers, and carried off
the oxen that were biding in the house. The
river Liffey rose against them, so they put their
garments on the horns of the oxen, and the oxen
with the garments turned back thence to the
place in which Brigid was biding.

Once Brigid went into Magh Lemna to converse

with Patrick. He was preaching the Gospel
there. Then Brigid fell asleep at the preaching.
Said Patrick: "Why hast thou fallen asleep?"

Brigid prostrated herself thrice and answered:
"It was a vision I beheld," said she.

"Declare the vision," said Patrick.

"I beheld," said Brigid, "four ploughs in the
south-east, which ploughed the whole island;
and before the sowing was finished, the harvest
was ripened, and clear wellsprings and shining
streams came out of the furrows. White garments were on the sowers and ploughmen. I
beheld four other ploughs in the north, which
ploughed the island athwart, and turned the
harvest again, and the oats which they had sown
grew up at once, and was ripe, and black
streams came out of the furrows, and there were
black garments on the sowers and on the
ploughmen."

"That is not difficult," said Patrick. "The first
four ploughs which thou beheldest, those are I
and thou, who sow the four books of the Gospel
with a sowing of faith, and belief, and piety.
The harvest which thou beheldest are they who
come unto that faith and belief through our
teaching. The four ploughs which thou beheldest in the north are the false teachers and the

liars who will overturn the teaching which we are sowing."

Once when Brigid was in Armagh two persons passed her, bearing a tub of water. They went to be blessed by Brigid. The tub fell behind them and rolled round and round from the door of the stronghold down to Loch Laphain. But it was not broken, and not a drop fell out. It was manifest to every one that Brigid's blessing was upon them. Thereafter Patrick said: "Deal out the water to Armagh and to Airthir."

And every disease and every ailment that was in the land were healed.

Brigid went into the district of Fir Rois to release a captive who was in the district. Brigid said to the king: "Lettest thou your captive out for me?"

The king replied: "Though thou shouldst give me the whole realm of Fir Breg, I would not give thee the prisoner. But lest thou shouldst go with a refusal, for one night thou shalt have the right to guard his soul for him."

Brigid appeared to the captive at the close of day, and said to him: "When the chain shall be opened for thee, repeat this hymn and flee to thy right hand." And so it was; and the captive fled at Brigid's word.

nce Brigid went over Sliab Fuait. There was a madman biding on the mountain who used to harry the congregations. When the nuns beheld him, fear and great dread seized them. Brigid said to the madman: "Since I have come to thee here, preach thou God's word unto us."

"I cannot," said he, "avoid ministering unto thee, for thou art merciful unto the Lord's household, both the miserable and the poor."

Then said the madman: "Love the Lord, O Nun! and everyone will love thee. Revere the Lord and everyone will revere thee. Pray unto the Lord, and everyone will pray unto thee."

Once her father entreated holy Brigid to go to the king of Leinster, even to Ailill, son of Dunlang, to ask for the transfer of the ownership of the sword which he had given to him for a time on another occasion. Brigid went at her father's command.

A slave of the king came to converse with

Brigid, and said: "If I should be saved from the bondage wherein I abide with the king, I should become a Christian, and I should serve thee and the Lord."

Brigid went into the fortress and begged two boons of the king, namely, transfer of the ownership of the sword to Dubthach and freedom to the slave.

"Why should I give that to thee?" said the king.

"Excellent children will be given to thee," said Brigid, "and kingship to thy sons, and heaven to thyself."

Said the king: "The kingdom of heaven, as I see it not, I ask it not. Kingship for my sons, moreover, I ask not, for I myself am still alive, and let each one work in his time. Give me, however, length of life in my realm and victoriousness in battle over Conn's Half; for there is often warfare between us."

"It shall be given," said Brigid.

And this was fulfilled; for through Brigid's blessing thirty battles were won before Ailill in Ireland and nine in Scotland. The Húi Néill invaded Leinster after his death. The Leinstermen carried his body to the battle, and their foes were at once routed before them.

Brigid was once with her sheep on the Curragh, and she saw running past her a son of learning; Nindid the scholar was he.

"What makes thee run so, O son of learning?" Brigid said, "and what seekest thou thus?"

"O nun," said the scholar, "I am going to heaven."

"The Virgin's Son knoweth," said Brigid, "happy is he that goes the journey, and for God's sake, make prayer with me, that it may be easy for me to go."

"O nun," said the scholar, "I have no leisure; for the gates of heaven are open now, and I fear they may be shut against me. Or if thou art hindering me, pray the Lord that it may be easy for me to go to heaven, and I will pray the Lord for thee, that it may be easy for thee, and that thou mayest bring many thousands with thee unto heaven."

Brigid recited a paternoster with him. And he was pious thenceforward, and he it is that gave her communion and sacrifice when she was dying. Wherefore thence it came to pass that the comradeship of the world's sons of learning is with Brigid, and the Lord gives them, through Brigid's prayer, every perfect good that they ask.

Brigid went to Bishop Mél, that he might come and mark out her city for her. When they came then to the place in which Kildare stands today, that was the time that Ailill, son of Dunlang, chanced to be coming, with a hundred horseloads of peeled rods, over the midst of Kildare. Then maidens came from Brigid to ask for some of the rods, and refusal was given to them. The horses were straightway struck down under their horseloads to the ground. Then stakes and wattles were taken from them, and they arose not until Ailill had offered the hundred horseloads to Brigid. And therewith was built St Brigid's great house in Kildare, and it is Ailill that fed the wrights and paid them their wages. So Brigid left as a blessing that the kingship of Leinster should be till doomsday from Ailill, son of Dunlang.

Once two lepers came to Brigid to ask for alms. There was nothing in the convent except a single cow. Brigid bestowed that cow on the lepers jointly. One of the two lepers gave thanks to the Lord, but the other leper was ungrateful, for he was haughty.

"I alone," said he, "have been set at nought as regards a cow. Till today I have never been

counted among Culdees and the poor and
feeble, and I should not be in partnership as
regards this cow."

Brigid said to the humble leper: "Stay here,
till something be found for thee, and let this
haughty leper go off with his cow."

Then came a man to Brigid having a cow for
her, and she gave it to the humble leper. Now
when the haughty leper went on his way, he was
unable to drive his cow alone; so he came back
to Brigid and to his comrade, and kept reviling
and blaming Brigid.

"It was not for God's sake," said he, "that
thou madest thy offering; but it is because of our
importunity and oppressiveness that thou gavest
it to me."

Thereafter the two lepers went to the Barrow.
The river rose against them. Through Brigid's
blessing the humble leper escaped with his cow
but the haughty leper fell with his cow into the
river and was drowned.

Once the queen of Crimthan, son of Enna
Cennselach, king of Leinster, came with a silver
chain as an offering to Brigid. The semblance of
a human shape was on one end of the chain and a
silver apple at the other end. Brigid gave it to the
virgins. The virgins stored it up without her

knowledge, for greatly used Brigid to take her wealth and give it to the poor.

Then a leper came to Brigid, and Brigid gave him the chain without the nuns' knowledge. When the virgins knew this they said with anger and bitterness: "Little good have we," say they, "from thy compassion to everyone, and we ourselves in need of food and raiment!"

"Ye are sinning," said Brigid. "Go ye into the church in the place where I make prayer, and there ye will find your chain."

They went at Brigid's word. Though it had been given to a poor man, the nuns found the chain there.

Once the Kings of Leinster came to Brigid to listen to the preaching and celebration on Easter Day. After the celebration was ended, the king fared forth on his way. When Brigid went to eat her forenoon meal, Lomman, Brigid's leper, declared that he would eat nothing until there was given to him the king of Leinster's armour, both spears and shield and sword. Brigid sent a messenger after the king. From midday till evening the king could not find his path and they did not advance one thousand paces: so the messenger came up and took the armour from him and bestowed it upon the leper.

Once Brigid beheld a certain man passing her with salt on his back.

"What is on thy back?" said Brigid.

"Stones," said the man. "They shall be stones then," said Brigid.

Straightway stones were made of the salt. The same man came again past Brigid.

"What is on thy back?" said Brigid.

"Salt," said he.

"It shall be salt then," said Brigid. Salt was at once made of the stones through Brigid's word.

Once two lepers came to Brigid to be healed of the leprosy. Brigid bade one of the two lepers to wash the other. He did so.

"Do thou," said Brigid to the other leper, "tend and wash thy comrade even as he has ministered unto thee."

"Save the time that we have seen," said he, "we will not see one another. What, O nun, dost thou deem it just that I, a healthy man, with my fresh limbs and my fresh raiment, should wash that loathsome leper there, with his livid limbs falling from him? A custom like that is not fit for me."

So Brigid herself washed the lowly miserable leper. Said the haughty leper who had first been cleansed from the leprosy: "Meseems," said he, "that sparks of fire are breaking through my skin." He was filled with leprosy from his crown to his sole, because of his disobedience.

Once when Brigid was going to the bishop to receive the Sacrament, a he-goat's head seemed to her to be in the Mass-chalice. Brigid refused the chalice.

"Wherefore dost thou refuse it?" said the ecclesiastic.

"A he-goat's head is revealed to me therein," said Brigid.

The bishop called the lad who had brought the credence-table, and bade him make his confession.

"I went," said the lad, "into the house wherein goats are kept, and I took a fat goat thence, and I ate up my fill of him."

The lad did penance, and repented. Thereafter Brigid went to communion and saw not the semblance again.

Once guests came to Brigid: noble and pious were they, even the seven bishops who are on the hill in the east of Leinster. Then Brigid ordered a certain man of her household to go to

the sea and catch fish for the guests. The man
goes, taking with him his harpoon; and a seal
chanced to come to him. He thrusts the seal-
spear into it, and ties the string of the spear to his
hand.

The seal drags with him the man over the sea
unto the shore of the sea of Britain, and, after
breaking the string, leaves him there on a rock.
Then the seal was put back with his spear in it,
and the sea cast it on the shore that was near to
Brigid. However the fishers of Britain gave a
boat to Brigid's fisherman, when he had told his
tales to them. Then he crossed the sea and found
his seal here on the shore of the sea of Leinster,
and took it with him to Brigid's guests.

In the morning he went over sea, and passed
again over the sea of Britain to Brigid at
midday. The guests and the rest of the host
magnified God's name and Brigid's through that
miracle and through that prodigy.

Once a certain nun of Brigid's community
conceived a longing for salt. Brigid prayed, and
the stones were turned into salt, and the nun was
cured.

Once a churl of Brigid's household was cutting firewood. It happened to him that he killed a pet fox belonging to the king of Leinster. The churl was seized by the king. Brigid ordered the wild fox to come out of the forest; so he came and was at his tricks and playing for them and for the king by Brigid's orders. When the fox had done his deeds, he went safe through the forest, with the host of Leinster, both foot and horse and hounds, pursuing him.

Once bishops came to Brigid and she had nothing to give them, the cows having been milked twice. The cows came a third time to the place, and the milk they had then was greater than every other milking.

Once Brigid had a band of reapers reaping. A rainstorm poured on the whole plain of Liffey, but not a drop fell on her field.

Now this was another of her miracles. She blessed the blind table-faced man, and gave his eyes to him.

Once Brigid went to the widow, who killed the calf of her only cow for Brigid, and burnt the beam of her loom thereunder. God so wrought for Brigid that the beam was whole on the morrow, and the cow was licking its calf.

Once Brigid and Bishop Eirc were in Leinster. Brigid said to Bishop Eirc: "There is battling among thy people, and today they contend."

Hearing this, a clerical student to Bishop Eirc's household said: "We do not think it likely," said he, "that that is true."

Brigid sained the eyes of the clerical student. Thereafter he said: "I perceive," said he, "my brethren slaying them now."

And he made great repentance.

Once Brigid was herding sheep. A robber came to her and took seven wethers from her. However the herd was counted, and through Brigid's prayer, the wethers were found complete.

Once a certain man of Brigid's household made mead for the King of Leinster. When they came to drink it not a drop was found, for it had been consumed before Brigid. Brigid arose to save the wretched man, and she blessed the vessels, and the mead was found in fullness, and that was a wonderful miracle.

Once the seven bishops came out of Hṅi Briuin Cualann from Telach na n-Espac, and they

found Brigid in a place on the northern side of
Kildare. Brigid asked her cook, Blathnait,
whether she had any food. She said she had
none. Brigid was ashamed not to have food for
the holy men, and she besought the Lord
fervently. So the angels told her to milk the
cows for the third time that day. Brigid herself
milked the cows, and they filled the tubs with
the milk, and they would have filled even all the
vessels of Leinster. And the milk overflowed the
vessels, and made a lake thereof, whence it is
called Loch in Ais, that is the "Lake of Milk"
today. God's name and Brigid's were magnified
thereby.

For everything that Brigid would ask of the
Lord was granted her at once. For this was her
desire: to satisfy the poor, to expel every
hardship, to spare every miserable man. Now
there never has been anyone more demure, or
more modest, or more gentle, or more humble,
or wiser, or more harmonious than Brigid. She
never washed her hands, her feet or her head
among men. She never looked at the face of a
man. She never would speak without blushing.
She was abstinent, she was innocent, she was
prayerful, she was patient: she was glad in God's
commandments: she was firm, she was humble,

she was forgiving, she was loving: she was a consecrated casket for keeping Christ's Body and his Blood: she was a temple of God. Her heart and her mind were a throne of rest for the Holy Ghost. She was simple towards God: she was compassionate towards the wretched: she was splendid in miracles and marvels: wherefore her name among created things is Dove among birds, Vine among trees, Sun among stars. This is the father of that holy virgin, the Heavenly Father: this is her son, Jesus Christ: this is her fosterer, the Holy Ghost: wherefore this holy virgin performs great marvels and innumerable miracles.

It is she that helps everyone who is in difficulty and in danger: it is she that abates the pestilences: it is she that quells the anger and the storm of the sea. She is the prophetess of Christ: she is the Queen of the South: she is the Mary of the Gael.

t is Colomb Cille that made this hymn for Brigid, and in the time of Aed, son of Ainmire, he made it. And this was the cause of making it. A great storm came to Colomb Cille when he was going over the sea, and he chanced to be in danger of the whirlpool of

Corryvreckan, and he entreated Brigid that a calm might come to him, uttering the words of this hymn.

Or it is Brocan Cloen that made it, and it was made at the same time as *Nichar Brigid buadach bith*.

Or it is three of Brigid's household that made it when they went to Rome, and reached Placentia. And a man of the people of the city came to them outside and asked them whether they needed somewhere to stay. They said that they did. Then he brought them with him to his house, and they met a student who was from Rome, who asked them whence they had come and why. They said that it was for guesting. "That is a pity," said he, "for this man's custom is to kill his guests."

And they learned then through the student's teaching that poison would be given to them in ale; and they praised Brigid that she might save them, and they sang this hymn to Brigid. Then they drank the ale with the poison, and it did them no harm. So the man of the house came to see whether the poison had killed them. And he beheld them alive, and he beheld a comely maiden amongst them. Thereafter he came into the house, and was seeking the maiden, and found her not, and he asked them: "Why has the maiden gone?"

And they said that they had not seen her at all. So chains were put upon them that they might be killed on the morrow unless they would disclose the maiden. But the same student came to them on the morrow to visit them and, according to the story, *et inuenit eos in uinculis, et interrogauit eos quomodo euaserunt et cur ligati sunt.* [and he found them in chains and asked them how they had been preserved and why they were chained up.]

Or it may be Brenainn that made this hymn. Now Brenainn came to Brigid to know why the monster in the sea had given greater honour to Brigid than to the other saints. So when Brenainn reached Brigid, he asked her to confess in what wise she had the love of God. Said Brigid: "Make thou, O cleric, thy confession first, and I will make mine thereafter."

Brenainn said: "From the day I entered devotion, I never travelled more than seven furrows without my mind being on God."

"Good is the confession," said Brigid.

"Do thou now, O nun," said Brenainn, "make thy confession."

"The Son of the Virgin knoweth," said

Brigid, "from the hour I set my mind on God, I never took it from Him."

"It seems to us, O nun," said Brenainn, "that the monsters are right, that they give greater honour to thee than to us."

Or it is Ultan of Ard Brecain that made this hymn for praise of Brigid. For he was of the Dál Conchubair, and so it was with Brigid's mother, Broicsech, daughter of Dallbronach. In the time of the two sons of Aed Slaine, this hymn was made. For it is they that slew Suibne, son of Colmán the Great, on one hand of Ultán. In Ard Brecain moreover it was made.

May Brigid, finest women, golden flame,
        delight,
    the sun dazzling, splendid, guide us to the
        eternal Kingdom!
May Brigid save us from throngs of demons!
May she wage before us the battle with all
        disease!
May she destroy within us all that taxes flesh!
Branch with blossoms, mother of Jesus!
True virgin, dear one, so dignified.
May I be safe always, with my saint of Leinster!
With great Patrick, one of the pillars of the
        kingdom,

the vesture over *liga*, the Queen of Queens!
Let our bodies in old age be in sackcloth:
May Brigid rain down grace on us and free us!

any miracles and marvels in that wise the Lord wrought for Brigid. So many are they that no one could tell of them all, unless her own soul or an angel of God should come to declare them. However this is enough as a sample of them.

Now when it came to Brigid's last days, after founding and helping cells and churches and altars in abundance, after miracles and marvels whose number is as the sand of sea or stars in the heavens, after charity and mercy, then came Nindid Pure-hand from Rome in Latium. The reason why he was called Nindid Pure-hand was that he never put his hand to his side, when Brigid repeated a paternoster with him. And he gave communion and sacrifice to Brigid, and sent her spirit to heaven.

Her relics are on earth with honour and dignity and primacy, with miracles and marvels. Her soul is like a sun in the heavenly Kingdom among the choir of angels and archangels. And though great be her honour here at present, greater by far will it be, when she shall arise like a shining lamp in completeness of body and soul at the great assembly of Doomsday, in union with Cherubim and Seraphim, in union with the Son of Mary the Virgin, in the union that is nobler than every union, in the union of the Holy Trinity, Father, Son, and Holy Ghost.

I beseech the mercy of High Almighty God, through holy Brigid's intercession, may we all deserve that unity, may we attain it, may we dwell therein *in saecula!*

Hail Brigid

The single remaining copy of this ninth century poem is found in the Book of Leinster. *It is an inaccurate and in many places illegible or unintelligible copy. The slightly shortened version given here is freely rendered and adapted from the editing and translation of Kuno Meyer, published in 1912, with the aim of recapturing some of the poetic rhythm and epic tone of the original.*

The poem's theme, as presented in Meyer's preface, is "the disappearance of the pagan world of Ireland and the triumph of Christianity, as exemplified by the deserted ruins of the ancient hill-fort of Alenn, contrasted with the flourishing state of the neighbouring Kildare."

In ancient times, the hill-fort of Alenn was the seat of the kings of Leinster. It was abandoned as a royal residence some time between the death of king Bran mac Connaill in 695, and the end of the eighth century. In the Prologue to the Félire *of the Irish poet, Oengus, written about that time, it is said:*

Alenn's proud citadel has perished with its warlike host!

We read in the Life of Brigid *how the then king of Leinster, Ailill, son of Dunlang, was obliged to help Bride build her convent at Kildare. He enjoyed her protection against his enemies and her blessing that the kingship should descend from his line "till dooms-day." This alliance proved invincible even after his death, when his body was brought to the battle and the invading Néill were routed.*

The unknown author of "Hail Brigid" invokes the proud roll-call of the warlike kings of Leinster and their brave deeds. But their power has now passed away and it is the "sovereign queen with gathered hosts" (Bride with the monks and nuns of Kildare) that now rules over all. The fine poetry and resounding images of this piece of writing, especially where it re-creates the splendour of Alenn at the height of its power, have a wonderfully epic quality.

rigid, sit thou enthroned in triumph
        upon the sweet plain of Liffey,
            as far as the strand of the
                ebbing sea!
    Thou art sovereign queen with
        gathered hosts
over all the sons of Cathair
        the Great.

Though the glittering Liffey is yours today
    this land fell to many before.
When I gaze over the fair Curragh,
    the fate of those fine kings fills me with awe.

Loegaire governed even to the sea,
    and Ailill Ane's was a mighty name.
The light-filled Curragh still stretches away
    but not one of those kings remains.

Fine Labraid Longsech is no more,
    having trod his thirty years,
since the days when in Dinn Rig
    he dealt doom to Cobthach the Slim.

Lorc's grandson, Oengus of Roirin,
    seized rule over all of Erin;
Maistiu of the freckled neck, son of Mug Airt,
    threw princes down in their graves.

Far-famed Alenn! Hill of delight!
    Many a prince lies under your borne.
Greater you grew than ever was dreamt
    when Crimthan the Victorious held throne.

Hear the victory shouts after each triumph
    rise from a shock of swords, mettlesome
        mass;
see the strength of your warrior-bands
    in the dark-blue battle array;
hear the note of your horns above hundreds of
        heads.

Hear the tuneful ring of your black bent anvils,
    the sound of songs on the tongues of bards;
see the ardour of your men in the mighty fray;
    the beauty of your women at the
        banqueting.

There was drinking of mead there in every
        homestead;
    there were noble steeds, numberless tribes;
the jingle of chains unto kings of men
    under bloody blades of five-edged spears.

Hear the sweet strains there at every hour;
    see the wine-barque upon the purple flood;
the shower of silver of great splendour;
    the torques of gold from Gaulish lands.

Even to the sea of Britain
    the renown of your kings sped like a star.
Lovely Alenn, mighty and strong,
    made sport of every law.

Bresal Brec, king over Erin,
    Fiachra Fobrec with his fierce bands,
Fergus of the Sea, Finn son of Roth;
    these all loved to dwell in high Alenn.

But your spells and auguries came to naught,
    all your omens betokening death;
seen clearly now, such things seem vain,
    for Alenn is but a deserted dun.

Cathair the Great, the finest of men,
    ruled over Erin of many hues;
he will not come forth from his rath again
    for all his glory has passed and gone.

Fiachna of Fomuin, glorious Bresal,
    governed the sea with showers of spears;
thirty kings ruled to the very ocean,
    conquering lands around Tara of Bregia.

Handsome Feradach in his finery
    surrounded by crested bands of men;
with his blue-speckled helmet, his shining
            cloak,
    many a king he overthrew.

Dunlang of Fornochta, a generous prince,
    he routed the sons of Niall.
Yea, though we sing these tales over and over,
    it is no longer the world that was.

Enna's grandson, Illann, with his tribe
    thirty times battled against king and king;
he was a rock against fear;
    not a host rode to him but with royal
            banners.

Ailill was one who dealt in favours,
    against him fierce and blood-dark hosts:
Cormac, Carbre, Colman the Great, Brandub,
    ships bearing whole armies of men.

Faelan the Fair was a model of princedom,
    and Fianamail with him, too;
Bran, son of Conall, with his grand deeds,
    was a wave beating on the cliff.

O Brigid, whose land I behold now,
    where all these have ruled in turn,
thy fame has outshone them far,
    thou art indeed over them all!

Thou rulest evermore with the King
    beyond the land where your body lies.
Grandchild of Bresal, son of Dian,
    Brigid, sit thou enthroned in triumph!